WHEN FOOTBALL SEASON TURNS YOU INTO HIS SIDE CHICK

LaTasha D. Miles

For more information regarding speaking events, public
appearances and special discounts on bulk purchases,
contact LaTasha Miles at ldmiles247@gmail.com. Please
enclose "Football Season" in the subject line. For more
information regarding the images, contact Rich Griffis at
www.richgriffis.com or rich@richgriffis.com.

The views expressed in this literary work are those solely of the author. In no way were any of the names, persons, institutions, businesses or organizations listed in this book influential on the thoughts, experiences, and opinions of the author, LaTasha D. Miles.

CONTENTS

Disclaimer: "When Football Season Turns You Into His Side Chick: The Ultimate Survival Guide for Relationships & Households" contains some content that is intended for mature audiences only.

Dedication

I dedicate this book in honor and in loving memory of the woman who taught me about God: my grandmother, Ms. Elsie Mae Miles. Your voice descended from heaven one night, and you encouraged me to take on this endeavor. I will never forget what you taught me or what you've done for me. It's been more than four years since you passed and I am still heartbroken about your death, but I know the Lord makes no mistakes. Grandma, I thank you for rescuing me when I needed you the most. We've had our conversations and just when I was about to give up on my quest to become a sideline reporter and sports anchor, you made sure I kept pushing and I hope to make you proud. I'm doing this all for you! Thank you for blessing me with your presence! I miss you and love you so much. Surely, courtside seats and tickets on the 50-yard line are great, but when I do make it as a sideline reporter and sports anchor, you'll have the best seat in heaven … looking down at me!

Rest in Paradise
Elsie Mae Miles
September 4, 1933 – April 30, 2011

In Memoriam

Rest in Paradise, to my uncle, Randy Montgomery
Chrisp. You were always into music and writing
songs. When I was a teenager, you were the reason I
started writing, including music. We didn't talk all the
time, but I remember, you told me to never stop
writing. Well, look at me now, Uncle Randy! You
started this and it may have been some of the best
advice I was ever given! I hope that I will do
something with those songs I wrote after this book
venture … just maybe! Thank you so much for getting
me started! I love you!

To Barry Tapp, "Uncle Barry" as I liked to call you.
We were always either eating together, laughing,
talking about hunting or talking about football. I had
some of my best times with you, especially around the
holidays, in the midst of football season. Despite all
you went through, you never complained and that's
something I always admired about you. It was a
pleasure to be around you and your presence is truly
missed. I love you!

To my cousin and hair stylist of 16 years, Davian Daye, who was definitely going on the road with me when I make it to the big time, in this field! You had one of the most dynamic and energetic personalities ever and you were so respected and loved! I don't have enough space to continue to write how much you meant to me and others. I will sum it up by saying, thank you for being you and for never changing for anyone! I love you and miss you so much. No one will ever take your place.

To a buddy of mine from high school, Patrick "Saint" Powell. Before the summer of 2013, I hadn't seen you since we attended Cummings High and that night I saw you, we tripped out like we were still a couple of teenagers. Throughout the summer, we communicated, and when I told you I was writing a book about football and relationships, you told me some of the most philosophical and encouraging words I had ever heard! At that time, I needed to hear it, because I was at a crossroads and really struggling and I sincerely appreciate it! I originally had you listed in the "Thanks and Gratitude" section and I hate that you didn't get to see my thanks to you, because you perished on November 11, 2013. However, because what you shared with me meant so much and it pushed me, when I do make it and when your son is ready to play some football, put me down for a pair of cleats, a jersey or something! I miss you and thank you so much! Your legacy lives!

To my beautiful, unique coworker and fellow *May Baby,* KiTonya Regan. You loved basketball just as much as I love football. We used to talk about how our passion and knowledge of the sports, and our Taurus instincts were going to help us take over the leagues. Thanks for making it so cool to be a female who loves sports, too. Your presence is truly missed!

To my coworker, birthday twin and buddy from "1902" who was just as passionate about football as I am, the avid, Mr. Akil Reginald Hamilton. It must be a Taurus thing and because we were born on May 9th! My birthday hasn't been the same since you perished and I appreciated your spirit more than anything! You just watch what I'm about to do for you when I really do make it, big homey! I've been talking to your father about this and you just wait and watch what's about to happen! Give me one or two years, Akil! I love you and miss you so much!

Thanks and Gratitude

I give all credit and praise to my Heavenly Father for blessing me, comforting me, guiding me, protecting me and strengthening me. I am a prayer warrior and I thank you, Father, for always being there for me. I have all faith in you and I thank you for what you have done, what you are doing and what you will do for me. I wouldn't be where I am today without you and I am extremely humbled and eternally grateful.

Just to think, this project started from posts on social networks on the first day of football season a few years ago and turned into my first book. My grandmother gave me the confirmation when her voice spoke to me from heaven one night and she told me to do it. This has taken a lot of work and a lot of time and effort, but it has also been so much fun to complete this book. It's a year overdue, and although I had my share of hiccups throughout this process, I'm not complaining, I've learned so much and I'm still satisfied with the outcome. Those obstacles truly taught me that without tests, there's no testimony, and a setback is a setup for a comeback. I appreciate it all, even the little things. And I have several (and I do mean several) people and organizations to show love, admiration, and thank for your contributions throughout my journey. I also encourage everyone: never give up on your dreams or yourself!

To the woman who gave me life, my ambition, my generous heart, my personality, my wit and my work ethic: my mother, Vanessa D. Miles. Without you, there's no me. I get only one of you and you're priceless. I love you and thank you for everything! Above all, I hope to make you proud! Sorry I haven't given you a grandchild ... yet! (OK, maybe I'm not *that* sorry). Thanks again for everything! I love you forever and always!

Thank you to all of my aunts, especially Ann Chrisp, Beulah Farrish, Deborah "Queen" Miles, Evelyn Miles, Geneva "The Diva" Miles, Patsy G. Miles and Virginia Walker. Thank you to all of my uncles, especially Vernon Chrisp, A.O. Miles, Gary Miles, Perry Miles and my honorary uncles, Perry Burton and Terry Scott. To all of my cousins, my "RAM FAM" and former classmates, my church family, my neighbors, additional family and friends, and to my coworkers for making it such a joy to come to work each and every morning! Thank you for your support, prayers and for believing in me!

I must also thank my cousin, Anthony W. Walker. Although we live in different time zones and regardless of what else is going on, we always manage to talk about football, games, highlights and the history of the game. Sometimes, I've even given you advice about your fantasy football rosters and I've laughed about that each time you've called with your questions. You've been very instrumental in why I love football as much as I do. I am incredibly proud of you and what you've accomplished out there in Colorado and wish you continued success! I love you "cuz" and thanks so much!

To one of my biggest supporters, my God brother and best friend of more than 14 years, Marcus Ellis Waldrum, who even came with me when I covered my first baseball game. You even stayed with me during that 50-minute rain delay to make sure I was OK and the next day … I had a front-page article! Do you remember that? And anytime I needed to talk to you about anything, even if it was at 1:30 a.m. and you had to wake up in a couple of hours for work, you were there for me. There were times when I wanted to give up and you made sure that I didn't. You always reminded me of my talents, my gifts and how beautiful I am inside and out, even when I didn't believe it myself. You help keep me grounded and our bond is unbreakable! We go above and beyond for each other, and people could learn so much from our friendship! I'm elated and so grateful to have you as my best friend! I love you to the moon and back, and thank you so much!

To Terri Ayawna Miller, "Tam" as I like to call you. Tam, you are the most beautiful and most profound 14-year old ever! You have inspired me in so many ways. I am in complete awe of you and know that I am always here for you! Proms, graduations, when you get your driver's license … you name it, I'm there! I love you so much and thank you!

To Doby "Edgar Allen Po'etry" Crawford, my homey since middle school, who is actually like a brother to me. Thanks for being my first responder when my grandmother passed and for making sure I had what I needed through this journey of writing my book. I appreciate you more than you'll ever know! You've always been a huge supporter and pushed me to get out of my comfort zone. I've thoroughly enjoyed watching your evolution, your transformation and your growth and I couldn't be more proud of you!

I don't know if you're passing me the baton or I'm passing it to you, but we're up next. And let's do something with those songs we wrote back in the day. Thank you so much and I love you!

To the stunning and talented, Tramiece McRae. I appreciate you so much! It's awesome to be around another female who is just as ambitious, charismatic, intelligent, lovely, and uplifting! We have such good times and laughs without all the bickering, jealously, and backstabbing that are common amongst some other females. You are so beautiful and I love your spirit! You've been so loyal and such an ambassador for me lately, and I don't know what I would've done without you! You are truly my friend. We need more like you. I love you dearly and thank you so much!

To my teachers, especially Mrs. Elizabeth Clark, now a senior lecturer in the School of Journalism and Mass Communication at Texas State University-San Marcos. Thank you for giving me my first official start in the world of sports journalism. In the midst of chasing my dreams, you helped me find my purpose in this field, and your efforts are appreciated more than you'll ever know. I also thank you for checking on me after your departure from Winston-Salem State

University and for assisting me on this journey. I miss you dearly and thank you so much, Mrs. Clark!

To the staffs of the *High Point Enterprise*, the *Winston-Salem Journal*, the Diversity Institute of Multimedia Scholars, the *South Bend Tribune* and *The News Argus* on the campus of my esteemed alma mater, Winston-Salem State University, for providing me with all of my opportunities that allowed my work to be published, land front-page articles, interview Hall of Fame members and win awards. I am tremendously proud to be a RAM!

To my fellow RAM, Brian "B-Daht" McLaughlin, thank you for your contributions throughout my process of writing this book and while I was on the radio. They were major! I've had the pleasure of witnessing your iconic evolution in media and I hope to follow in your footsteps. I'm so happy for you and proud of you, sir! Keep doing you!

To 102 Jamz, Mike Crenshaw, Alan Hooker, Walter T. Johnson, Guilford County Schools and tenwebtv.com in Greensboro, NC, for granting me additional outlets to broadcast about football. To all the coaches and players I've ever interviewed, thank

you! To my fellow North Carolinian and former
Tennessee Titans defensive line coach, Jim Washburn,
thank you for your assistance as well, during your
time with the Titans. You made a huge contribution to
my article! To my fellow RAM and fellow Taurus,
William Hayes, of the Miami Dolphins. I won my first
award covering a story about you, while you were
with the Titans. That gave me further confirmation
that the sports media realm is where I belong. I am
very proud of you and forever grateful.

To William E. Lee Jr., for your expertise and
resources. To Rich Griffis, for your vision, thank you,
thank you, thank you! I gave you very few directions,
and you created an amazing, timeless book cover I am
extremely proud of, and you should be too. You gave
my project its visual completion and I am truly
amazed by your talents. You were such a pleasure to
work with and I hope we will have more chances to
collaborate. Thank you! To Kiki Lowe, for refining
my project with the polish it needed and I thank you.
To my unsung hero throughout this entire process, my
attorney, Mr. Harold Hunter, Jr. Words can't express
my gratitude for you, sir. You are the best!

Special thanks to: Chip Adams, Danon Alston, Duane
Anderson, Ron Baldwin, David Bales, King Eric Bell,
Trevor Bethel, Steven Bowers, Rocky "Uncle Rock"
Brinkley, Dreama Caldwell, Ron Carthen, Jeremiah
Da Ré, Coach Stephen Davis, DJ Small Wonda, Ms.
Madeline "Sweet" Faucette, Todd Fox, my fellow
May 9th Taurus Sharon Fuller, Steve Genslak,
Kenosha Hall, Dr. Johnny Hamilton, Matthew Head,
Steve Johnson, Mo Kintu, Christopher "CB" Lea,
Bobby McFadden, Dale Miller, Terry Miller, Robert
Mitton, Rod Montaqué, Al Moseley, Darren Murray,
Stephanie Quadé, Eugene Rainey, Lekyvis Regan,
Rich Kid Radio, Steve Roberts, Versail Roddey, Ms.
Marilyn Roseboro, my photographers Deana Marshall
and Philshaunda Abdus-Salaam, Tamara Shanell,
Jerry Sumner, Vanessa Swing, Justin and Victoria
Thompson, Roland Trout, Glenn Van Natta, Todd
Whitley and Joni Winebarger. And to my "RAMily"
Jasmene Braden, Jerell M. Fields, James Geiser,
Melvin Hinson, Beverly Ramsey, Barry Summerour,
Alonzo Turner, Tristian Turner, Robyn Wiggins and
Byron Williams.

You guys came through in the clutch for me and I
thank you all so much! I'll never forget what you
contributed throughout my journey!

Much love to my brother Sedrick B. Bigelow, Jason Carey, my grandmother Linda Chrisp, my father Wilbert L. Chrisp, Jr., Alice Hess, my future sister-in-law Ebony Jackson, Kelly Johnson, my sister Ashley Lewis, Yvette Losaw, Rica Ross, Donza "Donzaleeza Rice" Slade, Ramona Smith, Gina Tapp, my adorable nephew Gracen "G-Money" Waldrum, the Chandler Family and all of my paternal family.

To the staff of Smokey Bones in Greensboro for your hospitality during football seasons in the past, thank you! Last but not least, thank you to the boys of "1902" and to the crew from Cut-N-Up Barber Shop formerly in High Point, NC. Thank you guys for inducting me into your "males only" clubs. I know it was against the typical macho man code, but then again, with my knowledge and passion about football, I guess I left you no choice, except to embrace me!

To Brandon Tate of the Buffalo Bills. I'm very proud of you and wish you nothing but continued success and many more blessings to come. I hope to see you on the sidelines one day soon. Keep representing Burlington, NC, to the fullest!

Who Am I?

I'm just a girl from Burlington, NC who loves football and I evolved into a woman who took a chance! I still can't believe that I actually wrote a book … Wow! I thank God endlessly for granting me with this opportunity and for providing me with the courage, the vision and the platform to take on this endeavor. Thank you to anyone who has ever listened to me on the radio, watched me on television or read any of my articles. I also want to thank the ones who didn't write me off or count me out, when the chips were down. Thanks to those who didn't abandon me and to whomever I forgot to name, please charge it to my head and not my heart. I tried to show love to those I know, who've shown me love and support, believed in me, been a positive influence for me, and encouraged or inspired me through this journey in my sports journalism career and in writing this book, either individually or collectively by group or association. I want you to see my appreciation for you and know that I am truly grateful and I thank each one of you! In some way, shape, form or fashion, big or small, each of you were a part of my journey. You all have a special place in my heart! Thank you and I hope you enjoy my book.

Preface

Award-winning sports writer and self-proclaimed "dainty tomboy" LaTasha D. Miles brings her experiences as a football sideline reporter and radio personality into this literary work. With an entertaining and insightful look into the dynamics of how and why relationships may change, "When Football Season Turns You Into His Side Chick" explains why a woman may feel like she has temporarily transitioned from the "main chick" to the "side chick" during this time of year.

From how to handle various situations in the world of watching football, like fantasy football and amusing anecdotes to some competitive scenarios such as who gets to watch the "big TV" while the games are on, this book will answer several penetrating questions including, "What is a side chick?" It will also open the lines of communication on how a man can successfully balance two of his loves ... his love for the woman in his relationship and his love for football.

"When Football Season Turns You Into His Side Chick" provides some assurance for the women, some explanation for the men, and some understanding for both genders. This collection of interesting tips and resolutions will prescribe the perfect balance on how to keep peace in your relationships and households ... well, at least during football season.

PRE-GAME COVERAGE

Pre-Game Coverage

Why does football season have the same level of anticipation and excitement for men as Valentine's Day does for women?

As if it isn't hard enough trying to maintain a relationship as complexities arise, Valentine's Day meets its most challenging opponent head-on: football season! It's the time of year when many women find themselves pushing up against a brick wall while seeking intimacy and conversation. Arguments are common, and neglect becomes familiar as relationships fight for survival.

A woman able to endure the emotional roller coaster of football season is one worth keeping around. Not only must she maintain her composure while meeting a few unfamiliar guests in the house, but her seasonal role as the "side chick" may take her on a journey of emotional discomfort. This is not the time to start throwing dishes or packing. Instead, it can be an awesome time to strategize a plan to get back in the driver's seat as his "main chick."

Rather than look at this season as a negative, make it a positive by learning your man's nuances and adjusting accordingly.

If you can find a relative from his side of the family to get on your side of a disagreement, then you should make it through football season with ease!

The main chick, who customarily receives gifts on Valentine's Day, looks forward to the arrangements of beautifully colored flowers and being pampered on that holiday, is the same chick who is easily demoted to "side chick" during football season.

How would one define a side chick?

Well, a side chick has a complicated, yet simple role during football season. A side chick knows her position, but she doesn't necessarily like it. Knowing that a man is already preoccupied and involved in a primary relationship (football), the side chick plays the secondary role, of being simply convenient. But when this time of year comes around, this example is the epitome of role reversals as football season emerges into a man's main chick and the primary woman becomes his side chick by default.

Although this definition of a side chick shouldn't be taken literally, some traits fit perfectly in outlining a man, his relationship with his lady and his obsession with watching football.

Let's not look at sex as the primary reasoning behind having a side chick. Can you remember the way you felt when he forgot Valentine's Day and didn't pick up that jewelry you'd been asking about for months? Well, ladies, that's how he feels when you forget how important football season is to him.

With less than two weeks separating the league's championship game and Valentine's Day, it's easy to see how heated these "holidays" can become. A man foresees his favorite team winning the title for the season, the same way a woman envisions being sent a surprise bouquet of red roses to her workplace, as a preview of what's to come for Valentine's Day.

During football season, your man has unique and special needs. He doesn't want to hear nagging or complaining about him not doing the chores. Nor will he be up for much conversation. He just wants to enjoy a cold brew and an accommodating atmosphere.

Men tend to form this bond with football early in life, by participating in the sport with other youngsters and/or watching the games with friends and family. While playing football, a fraternity builds; it's an unbroken brotherhood. It's the common denominator shared because they all understand the emotional, physical and mental sacrifices that arise from the camaraderie and experiences from playing on the gridiron. Your man acquires knowledge of the game and his passion for the sport develops. This eternal connection is like no other. Even as a lad, he posed in pictures often, in the stance of a player on the gridiron, with a football and helmet.

Because of his unrivaled attachment to football, talking trash about one of his earliest loves will quickly demote you to the sidelines. You have to be innovative, ladies, and get to the heart of what he loves!

His attention span will be shorter than usual during football season, so you have to become creative and make your point in a matter of seconds. Men typically get bored with emotional expressions, so sharing all of the long, deep, drawn-out details of your emotions may fall on deaf ears, especially during football season, and what woman wants that? He has a more complex bond with watching football, one that you may not ever understand. But you can still find a way to interact with him without losing your "main" position.

Oh yes, watching football definitely wins the battle and unanimously becomes his priority for a few months.

Your job, ladies, is to win the game on your own terms and finish emotionally unharmed. While his emotions are in a committed relationship with watching football, what's a woman to do? When you're planning to spend some quality time with him and he's planning a night out watching football with his buddies, how can you win? When you're planning on pulling back the sheets to watch a romantic movie with him and he's planning on pushing back in his recliner, enjoying a date with his remote to watch football, how can you win? When you're planning a candlelight dinner with the rich aromas of prime rib and robust wine and he's planning to watch the games while the smells of fried chicken wings and stale beer linger throughout your home, how can you win?

He becomes more involved in a love affair with the football games displayed on the television screen and less attentive to you, his significant other. You catch him rearranging his schedule around the football lineup, but he can't seem to remember to pick you up from work. You might even catch him rearranging his sleeping patterns around watching football. With bags sagging from his eyes, his pupils dilated from excitement and an energy rush, his focus is certainly not on the lover's lane you envision.

So, planning date nights while football is on television is unequivocally and legalistically out of the question! Unless you're committing yourself to actually attend a game or go out on a date to watch the games, good luck with that one. You've scored yourself a place in "side chick lane" longing for quality time and companionship. That feeling of *he'd rather watch the games, than spend some time with me!?!? Oh, he must be crazy!* Yeah, that's the familiar feeling.

Of course, this is not the case for every man or woman in their respective relationships, but speaking overall, a disconnection may occur amongst couples during this time of year.

The frustration a woman experiences tends to mount as football season is the culprit. Certainly, football season doesn't have as much meaningful value in a relationship as the vital intangibles such as trust, respect, loyalty and love, but it has its own special place and thusly, has to be handled with care as well.

Football season does not have to lead to a breakup, a separation or a divorce, although it might leave you feeling lonely and unappreciated. Because no woman wants to find herself at the bottom of her man's list of priorities, this book includes a few pointers to keep your position secure.

Certain segments of football season will matter more to him than others. If he misses the biggest game of the season, there's a pretty good chance your man will show some immediate signs of depression. Keep in mind that pre-season begins in August. Pre-season games are not as significant as the big game, but the side chick-versus-main-chick tension begins to take center stage in your relationships. And when the regular season kicks off in September, a bigger wedge may form within your relationships and households. The man you know and love will begin a transformation of sorts, becoming somewhat distant and he'll find watching football as an outlet to escape the madness of his days.

Meanwhile, you begin to experience feelings of neglect and disassociation. (I hate that I'm the sour grape to break it you, but football season is the one to blame for your honey's erratic behaviors.)

Surely, you can't blame football season for intentionally destroying your peaceful, happy home. Just remember, football season doesn't know any better and it's not on purpose, but there's just something about watching football that accelerates men and drives their adrenaline wild.

What you *can* blame football season for is bombarding its way into your living room without your expressed approval and stealing your man's attention. When football season intrudes, alienation of affection sets in, emotions run amok and your household turns into a simulated stadium, where it's you and him on opposite sides of the playing field.

Men don't necessarily intend to mishandle your feelings and demote you into the role of the side chick. The most important thing to remember is, to never panic and never say things you don't mean. Your man will return to reality soon, and the love you once knew will rekindle. This is not the time to get aggressive and emphasize your feminine right to scream at the top of your lungs. It's the time to get educated and learn some offensive and defensive tactics.

No need to fret and call a timeout to complain to your girls, either, because this book will help answer your burning questions and give you tips on how to stay cool, calm and collected. It's your play-by-play analysis for your relationship during the season. And while this is not a book outlining the official rules and regulations of football, it will alert you to the common behaviors evident during the season. You'll learn how to address those behaviors, and you'll know that you're not alone.

Pouting and complaining during this time of year, and anticipating the season's departure may extend your misery. Instead, show some excitement. Football season can be fun, and it may actually bring you and your lover so much closer, rather than tearing the two of you apart.

This book aims to explain why women get temporarily, *emphasis on temporarily,* pushed from the driver's seat in their relationships, into the passenger's seat, during football season. You will find assurance from another woman, with a feminine touch, explanation without excuse on behalf of the men, and an avenue to get positive dialogue going between you and your partner about this wonderful season called football!

This is, by no means a relationship intervention handbook or a tool to get in good with the guys, nor will this book guarantee you a trip down the aisle draped in a wedding dress. However, you should certainly use the information in this manuscript. Use it as a guide to navigate your relationship through the bumps and bruises that football season can inflict on your relationships your households. *When Football Season Turns You into His Side Chick: the Ultimate Survival Guide for Relationships & Households During Football Season* can ensure peace in your relationship and household ... well at least from September - February.

01

When September "Falls" On the Calendar

When September "Falls" On the Calendar

The autumnal equinox is upon us as we bask in the heat of mid-September. Cooler nights and more comfortable humidity pierce the dread of the summer's high temperatures. Beautiful fall foliage replaces the haze of the summer sun and the children return to school. Nevertheless, for most male football fans – and with all due respect to the month of December, with its festivities and collection of holidays – September is the best time of year, because football season returns.

One of the first things to understand other than the quarterback is one of the most integral positions, is that watching football is considered a sanctuary for many men. This may seem hard to believe with all the aggression, grunting, tackling and injuries, but it's true that even if he doesn't know football …

he *knows* football! Nothing is more relaxing to a

man on Sundays during football season than

cuddling up to his recliner in front of a large, flat-

screen TV with his favorite beer snuggled in the

palm of his hand. See ladies, men really do enjoy

cuddling and snuggling!

During this time of year, the man in your

relationship transforms into multiple characters.

Half of them may be new to you. Your honeybunch

becomes more than just a "football fan," and I

wouldn't dare suggest you use those two words

together in a sentence when referring to him,

because in most cases, his zeal goes way beyond

that title.

Although it has often been said that men can't

multitask, football season proves otherwise. As a

game gains momentum, a man also becomes a

coach, a player, a coordinator who calls the plays, the offense, the defense, the general manager, the team owner, a referee, a sports journalist, a reporter, a statistician, a football guru, and last but not least … a couch potato! Some of his actions, or lack of actions, may have you feeling like the side chick because his attention diverts to watching football. Am I right?

You're so tired of being ignored as the television volume soars, but rather than mope and lose interest, this is your prime time to dive into "assistant coach" mode. This is the best time to show him what *else* you're working with. There are ways to get sexy during football season without killing his testosterone rush.

You can assist him by making sure that the cable TV company he's using is giving him the best possible deal on football packages, and the bill is paid up to balance. Sometimes, the worst and least expected does happen: The room grows dim, the lights go out, the satellite system or cable shuts down and panic ensues, because he's unable to watch football. A man loves a sensible woman who can catch a great deal, and if you're able to do, especially with football, that's bonus points for you.

Does he happen to be scheduled for work during the time his favorite sport is on TV? Don't sweat it! Just take advantage of the amenities that come with your packaged deals and record the game(s) for him. Sure, he can watch the highlights, that's great ... but sit back and watch his face gleam as he realizes he didn't miss the games after all. And it's all because you took the initiative to record them for him to watch at his convenience.

Now that the television works and the cable is set to record his favorite moments, it's time to gather his accessories. Just as we have our accessories (and ladies, you know how much we love those … the purses, the jewelry, the shoes) … well, in the world of watching football, a key accessory for a man is that TV remote.

He will also need a recliner or his favorite spot on the couch, some sports-related magazines in the bathroom, snacks, drinks, a spare set of batteries and his phone is optional. These are small details, but important ones, especially the batteries. Sadly, a man can become irate, if he actually has to get up and adjust the channel and/or volume for himself. You don't want him to have to get up and do that, do you? And you definitely don't want to force him to go to a bar or a buddy's pad to catch the games or highlights. Just allow your man to relax and enjoy the games!

Are you finding that you're not savvy when it comes to technology, and that you're impatient with waiting for customer care services? Not a problem at all! Just turn this adventure into a shopping extravaganza and you'll find yourself right at home.

Here's a task for you: Find out who is his favorite player or team. See if you can't surprise him with the perfect football jersey, a hat, a pair of lounge pants, a scarf, or anything symbolic of his favorite player or team. If you're unsure because you're in a new relationship or you haven't been paying much attention to this stuff, enlist family and/or friends to get the scoop on what he likes. In a world where gift cards have become more convenient but impersonal, what better way to show him you care?

For maybe the first time in a woman's relationship, he won't mind if you investigate, and playing the detective role can prove to be advantageous. Look in his closet at other hats, shirts and jerseys to find his sizes. Don't start feeling guilty; you're on a mission to gather some important evidence!

Are you chummy with his family? Well, ask one of his relatives who his favorite player or team is, as this will heighten the surprise. Make sure he keeps the frumpy team paraphernalia at home to support his superstitions, but if you buy him a jersey or hat, make sure it's one he can show off to his pals.

A few suggestions: license plate holders, ink pens, toothbrushes, and beer canisters and other goodies embossed with team logos. The possibilities are endless, and his passion for the game gives you just the right reason to spend some money. The power of a personal gift is priceless, so you don't want to let this opportunity pass you by and miss that surge of his adrenaline. A personal gift sends a personal message. It shows exclusivity and lets him know that you're watching. If you prefer a gift that doesn't require as much research, then pick up a football-related video game that corresponds with his video game console and get yourself a tight-fitting skirt to include his gift box!

You're taking an approach that your man will find incredibly sexy, and you didn't even have to remove your clothes! The translation to your man is, "I went out and specifically got you something special, honey. This gift belongs to you!"

Actually, it might surprise you at how much fun shopping for football paraphernalia is and how far these examples of "assistance" will go for you.

Go ahead and keep picking up a few little somethings for yourself, too. Or throw it on a list for him to pick up, and everyone remains a winner.

Because merchandise is also available with team logos for babies and children, you can dress up the entire family, take some unique studio portraits, frame one for his desk, and send them to family and friends.

Speaking of team dedication – and I'm speaking to just the men here – just because you raise your child or children to be loyal to your favorite team and dress them up in jerseys like yours, when they grow up, they *can* change their minds. They might move to another city and root for the local team or grow to become a fan of a player on another team, and consequently root for that squad. You can't force them to keep liking a team just because you do. However, you can expect your child or children to jump ship if that team is a losing franchise. Ultimately, the choice is theirs.

Now, back to the ladies. Instead of dreading September's arrival, consider how these examples can get the month started on the right foot. While you're school shopping for your children during this time of year anyway, you might as well pick up some attire with team logos on it and take care of the "big kid" in your household, too.

02

When His Fantasy Doesn't Include You

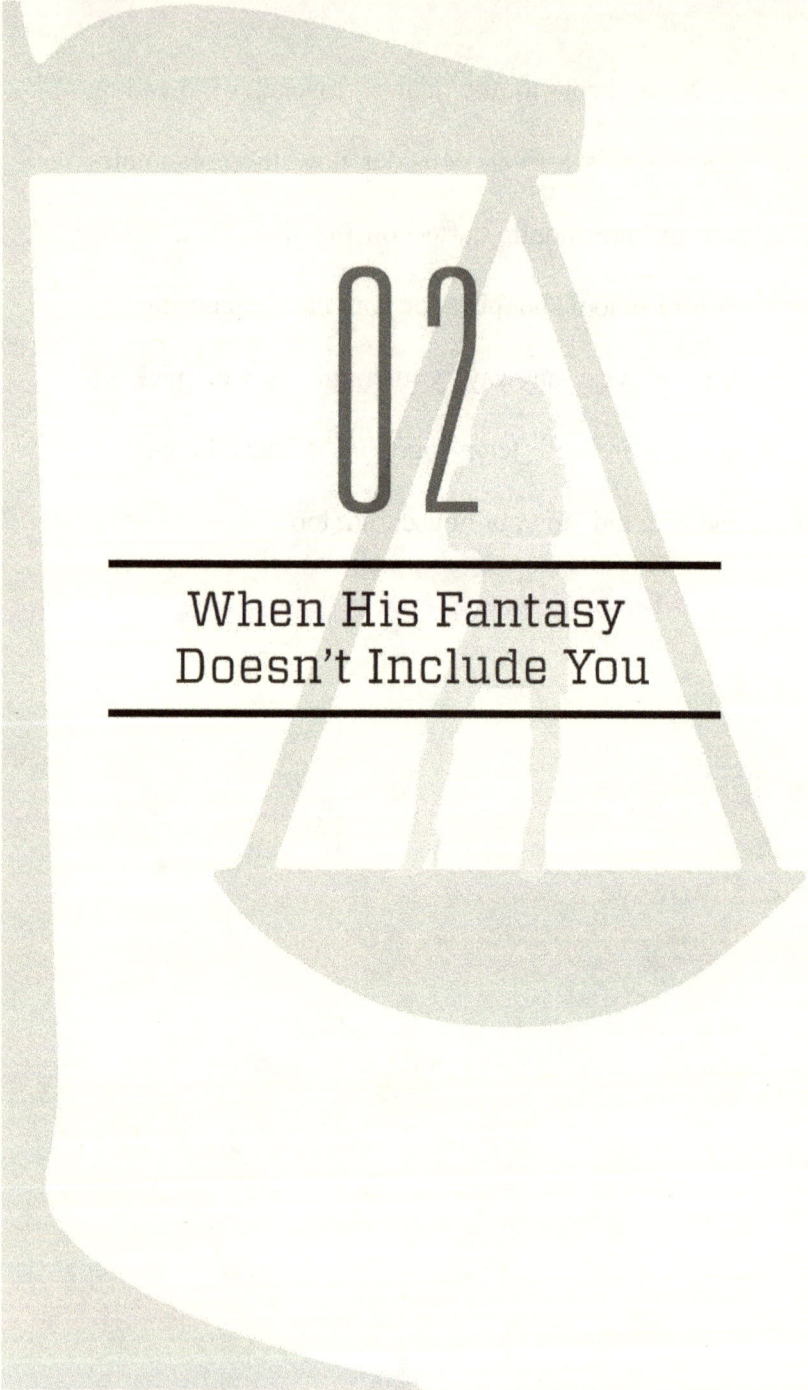

When His Fantasy Doesn't Include You

Ladies, there's no way around the fact that men fantasize about a lot of different things, from money to women to fast cars, even to women washing those fast cars (in minimal attire, of course). However, there's another fantasy trend that's captivating your man's sensuality: fantasy football. The popularity of playing in fantasy football leagues has its own unique allure and has grown immensely from its humble beginnings in the 1960s.

Back in the day, fantasy football plays were often submitted through the newspaper, but with the expansion of the Internet, it has catapulted into an addictive enjoyment for many men. The perks to playing along through December or early January may include bragging rights for a season, earning trophies and, the most important part ... winning money.

Don't panic ladies, because this type of web-based fantasy is really nothing to get concerned about. The only women involved in these fantasies are those like me who just love football, and we play along in fantasy leagues. We only want to defeat the guys, bruise their male egos, and poke fun at them about our victory when it happens.

While playing in fantasy leagues, you run the operation of your own football team, like a general manager would. It's not the act of fantasizing about other women and the actual stigma associated with the word, when a woman hears that her man was involved with or had a *fantasy*.

Sure, playing football or coaching a team is fun, but being able to draft and manage your own roster of players gives you an instant rush of adrenaline. By participating in fantasy leagues, your man is granted that opportunity. Your significant other gets to manage his own virtual football team consisting of the league's top players of the various positions. This occurs by drafting players for several rounds, trading players, adding and dropping players throughout the season, and by adjusting the rosters once their draft is completed.

Once the draft is finished and the season begins, each general manager's team will face an opposing general manager's team weekly within that fantasy league. It is the responsibility of each general manager to make the correct selections within his or her roster, in an effort to determine who will most likely bring home a win for the week.

Please note that these adjustments in his team roster will occur weekly. The football league's regular season lasts for 17 weeks (including a bye week for each team, and the teams actually play 16 games each. Fantasy football doesn't generally include the football teams' playoff games).

Depending on whether his league begins the first week of the season in early September, how it's set up and how his fantasy league's playoffs system works, you should expect your significant other to be involved with this activity and most likely, emotionally unattached for about 12 to 17 weeks.

Just a heads up, your male counterpart might also participate in multiple fantasy football leagues. You may find him rooting for and against the same player, because he may have that player on his team in one league, but playing against him in a different one. Also, and I know this might seem strange, but there may even be a time or two when he may not want a player from his favorite football team to do so well, and that's because his competition in the fantasy league(s) might have that player as a member of their fantasy roster(s).

Nonetheless, here's another chance to prevent getting thrown into the side chick role and assist him. It wouldn't hurt to remind him to set his fantasy roster(s), especially on a Sunday at 12:35 p.m. Eastern Standard Time (since the first session of games begins at 1 p.m., and 12:50 or 12:55 p.m. is usually the latest that a roster for those earlier games can be updated). If he overslept, wake him up to set his fantasy roster(s), or if the religious activities you participate in remain in service when the games come on, remind him earlier in the day to do so. Find out who is suggested to start in fantasy leagues that week and who should remained benched. You can even watch for higher-profile players on the injury list, because the worst phrase a man can hear during the fantasy period is *out for the season.*

In that case, especially if it pertains to him losing one of his early-round draft picks to injury for the remainder of the season (or if he loses a player due to a suspension), there is no doubt you will hear grunts of disapproval and/or profanity. Stand clear; he's about to start scampering for a replacement by attempting to trade other players on his roster(s) or checking within the fantasy league's free agency pool(s). He will receive information regarding breaking news and injuries, so it may not be necessary to report all the details happening around the league; however, your acts of assisting, being proactive and showing interest, are appreciated and actually give him another reason to be turned on by you, his main chick. Fantasy drafts can take place in a live format online, set up for automatic drafting, over the phone, or handwritten and entered into the computer by the league's commissioner, upon completion of the draft. Here's one thing I'm certain will happen: your significant other will want to attend one or more fantasy football draft parties, and these occur in mid – to – late August or early September. That can sound misleading, *a fantasy football draft party.*

This will not be a party per se. For the most part, the atmosphere will not be that of a party or a cookout, and there won't be a spread of various delicacies. No music, family and/or your friends, either. At most, the host might have some beer and wings at the venue to offer, but that's only a possibility. Most likely, it will be a "bring your own" food and beverage type of event, or the draft party might take place at a pub or restaurant. If you're not invited to this party, don't be offended.

Trust me: he's doing you a favor! It will look like a war room for 1 to 2 hours in someone's living room, pub or restaurant, with an uproar of competitive banter, lots of phones, laptops and magazines, with the exclusive purpose of strategizing the fantasy football draft(s). If you arrive with him to the draft party/parties, his buddies will definitely give him the "dude, you brought your lady" facial expressions and remarks, and he'll never hear the end of it from them.

You're not missing anything special, but if you must attend, bring your own music and headphones, your own magazines, some nail polish or something, because if you aren't drafting, you will be bored. Unless you have a good friend who is attending as well, or some type of activity to keep you occupied, you will not be entertained! Surely, the drafting process can take place in isolation, but there's just something about the camaraderie of hanging with others who share this common factor with you, desiring to have the same players on your virtual football team. From laughing at the bogus picks someone else makes or the use of profanity and the grunts of disapproval when somebody picks the player(s) you want on your team(s) before your opportunity is available, these factors add an extra dimension to the drafting process. Men (and women) get seriously involved in the art of fantasy football, and attending a draft party enhances this experience.

Therefore, when you hear he's going to a fantasy draft party or playing fantasy, as long as he's telling you the truth, it has nothing to do with sex or fantasizing about other women. It is with great pleasure that I inform you ... no assumption could be further from the truth.

03

When Home is His Second Castle

When Home is
His Second Castle

A gigantic, flat-screen television in your household is not required, but if there has ever been a question whether one should be purchased, let me resolve that for you: Absolutely! According to an A.C. Nielsen Co. survey conducted in 2012, the average American household owned 2.24 televisions.

If one of them is not a flat-screen television, then you have some shopping to do, especially during football season. A few years ago, the price of flat-screen televisions might have caused you to raise your eyebrows, but now that they are less expensive and in higher-definition, even watching commercials and cartoons on a larger platform is more entertaining. Whether it's a symbol of social status, or just the lure of "the bigger the screen, the better" or, hey … even for compensation purposes (shrug), men love to watch football on a large, flat-screen TV, and multiples ones if they are available.

Regardless of whether a man has ever touched the football field or played on a professional team and got cut, coached, played football when he was younger, injured, or received accolades for his playing ability – or perhaps he was just the water boy – when the games are on, your man automatically becomes the best thing that's happened to football.

In his mind, if a play goes wrong and if he was the team's coordinator instead, he would've called a better play. Or if a player is a bust, and your man was the team's general manager instead, (in his mind), he would've drafted a better player. Or even if a player with 4.2 speed, who catches 100 passes a season, drops a potential touchdown in the end zone – and your man was in uniform instead – he would've been a better option. Let me repeat that! *Or even if a player with 4.2 speed, who catches 100 passes a season, drops a potential touchdown in the end zone – and your man was in uniform instead – he would've been a better option.* Yeah, that guy who can perfect running routes on the football field and runs a 40-yard dash in 4.2 seconds, was the dummy for dropping the football in your man's mind, because somehow, someway, your man wouldn't have dropped it.

When plays go wrong on the field, nothing allows a man to effectively communicate these messages of frustration better than yelling at a larger-than-life, flat-screen television.

An even bigger bonus is if that TV is in his "man cave." Don't cringe so quickly, ladies! With the raucous activity, potential messes and *aromas,* the idea of him having a personal dwelling to watch football may actually be a bonus for you as well.

The man cave serves as a home away from home for a guy. It allows him to do what he likes without being bothered (still with some limitations, of course). He can decorate it however he pleases, with no interference from a female, and it doesn't throw the décor off balance from the other rooms in the house. He is free to relax and unwind without outside worries. It's the equivalent of boys having tree houses, but with more technology, a fridge and alcoholic beverages.

His sanctum is usually an extra bedroom in the home, the garage, the basement, the attic or the media room where he can have his buddies over to watch the games. Now if you are permitted into his private retreat during football season while the games are on, that's kind of like when your significant other gives you his last piece of food to show how much he loves you. There's no room for the "side chick" label if this happens, but confirmation is necessary. Make sure that his choice to let you in his man cave is carefully considered and not because he knows he will later regret the decision. Make sure he *really* means it.

A few essential items that you'll usually spot in his manly domain are lounge chairs, sports magazines, team posters, jerseys, food, beer, more beer and, of course, the flat-screen television. If you already have at least two televisions within your household, the largest one with the best sound and picture quality should be reserved for watching football on Sundays. Do whatever the rest of the days, but at least let him have Sundays to look at the games on that larger flat-screen, "Sunday-best" television.

And ladies, if you must watch your reality TV episodes, sitcoms, movies or recipe shows on other networks on Sundays, please do so in front of another television (preferably the smaller one), in another room with the door closed and/or the volume at a non-surround sound level.

But be forewarned; you're probably not going to be able to hear your shows or movies with all the play-by-play action, commentary and his hooting, hollering and carrying on from the other room. Working toward an exit strategy on Sundays during football season is not a bad idea at all.

04

When Sundays Arrive

When Sundays Arrive

Sunday, better known as the day of Sabbath, is the most important day of a man's week during football season. As a favor, ladies, also put nagging to rest on Sundays during this time of year.

Here's a reminder of this one important aspect to watching football: it's his sanctuary! After all, there are six other days in the week to return to your regularly scheduled nagging.

He may be hanging around lounging all day, running up the electricity bill, eating all the food, drinking all the beverages, but hey … at least he's home. If *you* don't want to be around, while all this football hoopla is occurring, this is a perfect day to go into another room, catch up on sleep, or go out and get a spa treatment. In fact, while he's waiting for the games to come on, he may be in a vulnerable state of mind. Consider this: you need pampering. He's preoccupied with his buddies and distracted, so this is an ideal time to ask him for a few dollars!

Ladies, you can also catch up on some reading, go to a library, attend book club meetings, do some gardening, go to the movies, participate in community and/or religious activities, go shopping, or even hang out with your family and friends. You don't have to necessarily do any household chores on Sundays, either. Take a break too, and fold that laundry on Monday!

While you're out and about – and if you plan to return home before the games are over – pick up some of his favorite beer. Sure, he'll already have plenty, but going on a beer run, especially since you're already out, is a bonus and he will appreciate your gesture of catering to him. And, this caring act will further solidify your spot as his main chick.

Whether he's participating in fantasy leagues, or competing along with his favorite team in a critical game – or other high-stakes situations – those 17 Sundays during the regular season are important to him. Tread lightly.

Consider this: When you buy more shoes and add to your collection, he helps you haul those bags in from the department stores, right? Or, let's say, he finds your secret stash of footwear in the back of the closet, or in a secret closet or under the bed. He knows better than to say anything about it so choose your battles wisely. He knows he's picking a fight if he makes any comments about your shoe purchases. Well, watching football on Sundays is his "shoe closet moment" … this is his equivalent of a "Valentine's Day" celebration.

I'm going to let you in on a little something that is probably the biggest reason football season matters so much, and why men cherish every opportunity to watch the games: its short season.

Of all the major professional sports, football has the shortest season of the year and the longest offseason.

Typically, football season officially begins on the Thursday following Labor Day, and the regular season ends during the last week of December or first week of January, depending how the dates fall on the calendar. Teams continue to play through January and into the first week of February, in the championship game, depending on how they fare in the postseason/playoffs. So his favorite team may even be out of the rankings within four months. That's less than half the year for him to enjoy one of his first and favorite loves – and for you to sacrifice your sanity!

By contrast, basketball season for example, begins in late October or early November, and it doesn't end until June. Baseball season begins in late March or early April and ends in October. Hockey season lasts from October until June, including playoffs. Auto racing begins in February and ends in November.

Summer comes and goes swiftly, but when you're a man eager to watch the games, summer is just another long, humid waiting game.

While anticipating the return of the season, your man will possibly become consumed with playing football-related video games. This keeps him occupied (and it can assist in keeping him away from other women). Add an ingredient of fun by joining in and playing the video games along with him. You don't have to be a professional at playing these games, but your enthusiasm brings another element of attraction he will have for you, in your continuous effort to secure your spot as his main chick.

By replacing any misplaced or broken games, you earn even more points. He enjoys playing as the season approaches, because these video games are therapeutic for him. He has a handful of football-related events to placate his anticipation, but they're sporadic, and they pale in comparison with the actual season.

For instance, in February to seek headlines from the scouting combine, in March for the excitement of free agency and the anticipation of who will go where; during the draft in April or May. In July, he has training camp and a couple of sports awards shows that display some football. Other than those highlights, the offseason is lackluster.

Therefore, he plays video games, which serve as a kind of antidepressant. You may also find him watching other sports to pacify his anticipation as he counts down the days as August and September approach. He'll definitely tune in to the pre-season games as an appetizer.

Sunday is the one day out of the week during football season when he needs watching the games as his asylum.

Seriously, Sundays during this time of year can feel like there are only 20 hours in a day. I assure you, ladies, football season goes by fast, and it's over before you know it.

Men should also be allowed their outdoor chores such as yard work and anything associated with auto mechanics as a part of the day of rest, too. Now this definitely is not an opportunity for lazy Sundays. The woman in the relationship can't be handling things at home all week and receive minimal assistance from her male counterpart. It is also the man's responsibility to get those things done during the week or early on Saturdays. This avoids consequences for not getting these tasks done around the house in order to lay around all day in your lounging attire, jerseys and hats on Sundays.

By the way, there is nothing wrong with your man cooking on Sundays during football season, so feel free to let him prepare your favorite meals. There's an additional level of attraction about a man who cooks.

When it was suggested that the woman assist with making football season more enjoyable by making sure your man has what he needs, food wasn't mentioned and that was intentional. This is not to exclude the importance of getting food, buying wings or cooking and preparing dishes for your man, but allow me to explain.

He's probably going to be lounging around the house most Sunday mornings during the season, and you might be participating in religion-related activities before the games come on TV. It's only fair that he prepare dinner, throw something on the grill or at least place a takeout order of food for the both of you. Guys, don't just take the food out the fridge and let it thaw out, that doesn't count. Wash the food, season and marinate it; even if you're not going to cook. Whoever cooks should be able to rest while the other washes the dishes, or that task can be shared. It's only fair. If you share the task, then it's the perfect time to catch an intimate kiss, share a dirty joke or splash water on each other. Make the kitchen your playground, and expand your sexual imagination.

Another note to the guys – do not use watching the football games as an excuse to abandon your normal religious activities. It's tempting to look at all the pre-game action dedicated to football on Sundays and find yourself mesmerized. You can and should still watch that action, but also remember to keep your lady happy by attending worship services as you usually do. The preacher will probably cut the sermon short on game days, and your main chick will leave you in peace to watch your games. As a matter of fact, I know a pastor who begins service at 10 a.m., and he concludes just in time to get home and enjoy the football festivities for the rest of the day. Of course, his members, who are also elated football fans, compromised and agreed to this time change, as well.

You can also attend other religious activities during the week, such as Bible Study. This suggestion applies especially to those outside the Eastern Standard Time zone. I have no recommendations for you all on Sundays, though, when it comes to balancing of praise and worship services with watching football. The games come on before 1 p.m. in your regions. Keep doing whatever you've been doing. The only thing I can suggest to you is … just wake up!

In all seriousness, the one thing that's certain is, do not turn in your religion card or sacrifice any religious beliefs on Sundays, simply to watch football. You can make some adjustments by opting to attend earlier services, or even online worship services.

Personally, I make it all come together on football Sundays by attending 8 a.m. services, then eating breakfast and proceeding to workout. I simultaneously exercise and watch the pre-game shows associated with football. I even set my fantasy rosters from my phone while I'm working out, because I'm able to watch TV and see the injury reports and segments that discuss which players to start on my fantasy teams.

For the Sundays that I don't tailgate and/or attend football games, I complete my workout, then return home by noon, get dressed (wearing sports paraphernalia embossed with my favorite team's logo, of course) and watch the games at neighborhood sports bars. This way, I get to praise, worship, and workout, in addition to getting my football fix, and all with a successful balance.

In addition to not abandoning your religious obligations on Sundays, remember that the household continues to have needs, and it still has to run properly. Household tasks don't disappear just because it's football season, so ladies, don't let him use "I'm watching the games" as an excuse. Guys, if you get everything taken care of before the games come on, you should at least be allowed to put reality on pause for the day.

Remember men, only you can prevent nagging!

05

When the Games
Come On

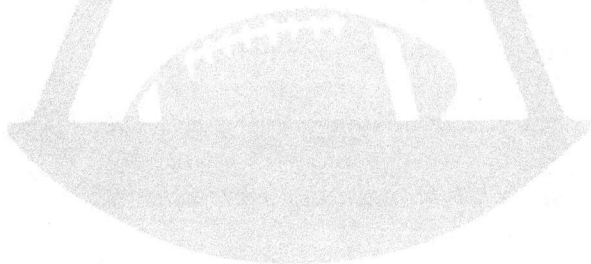

When the Games
Come On

All right, it's time to watch football; and ladies, I apologize for the inconvenience, and much to your chagrin, this is an *all-day* event. Even after the games conclude, there are highlights and post-game coverage on TV. It may seem a little overwhelming for you, so enjoy your male-free day at the spa or shopping mall. Or do what I think is the best option: skip the spa and watch the games with your guy.

I know what you're thinking: *Now why would I watch football with him and I don't even like it?* I can't blame you for having those thoughts, especially if football season makes you miserable. Your male counterpart can't change you and neither can I, but to be completely honest, watching football isn't that bad, especially once you gain an understanding of it. You may go from having the "He didn't have to hit him that hard" reaction to "Wooooo! Now that's how you tackle!"

Let me give you some motivation as to why you should watch football. First of all ladies, let's be frank about what you'll have as your personal viewing pleasure: MEN! Not only that but men wearing spandex pants!

Yeah, I know it's hard to see how some of these football players look because they're wearing helmets. Even when they're captured on screen without their helmets, some of these men don't always get their full justice of how incredibly handsome they are. There will be some heavy breathing, they'll be sweating and have a case of "helmet-head" but remember, these are football players and they are on the job. For the most part, these are some good-looking men, with chiseled bodies, and physiques akin to Greek Gods. Those uniforms put a huge emphasis on their lean, muscular physiques. The bonus is when the cameras go into the locker rooms for reactions after the games from the players and coaches. Be prepared, ladies, to tilt your head, raise your eyebrows and perhaps even bite your bottom lip as these enticing shots fill your television screens.

Now men, don't envy these football players when your woman is looking at them with wide eyes. But do catch some inspiration and take some notes on how to achieve those toned bodies. And ladies, don't even feel bad for looking at the football players with glares of temptation. Just because you're in a relationship, you're not oblivious to other attractive men. Even when you're on a diet, you can still look at the menu.

It's called guilty pleasure!

What I've noticed about my own love for football is that it has grown enormously over the years. At first, I hated the sport, but it was because I didn't understand it. That is so often the case with other situations in life. We are generally inclined to fear the unknown or what we don't understand. Other women have confessed that they also hated football initially, but it was only because they didn't understand the plays and the game was too fast and too complicated to understand.

There's no doubt that your male counterpart can also make it somewhat difficult to understand football, so naturally, you'll want to steer away from wanting to watch the sport. In addition, he can sometimes make you apprehensive if you want to ask him for some understanding.

I have to call the men out on this one. Now, you know, when your lady asks something about football – and depending on what questions she asks – you sometimes send a nonverbal message, along with a facial expression that tells her you don't want to be bothered.

It's the response in your tone, your body language and even the faces you make. Whether you respond this way on purpose, these reactions are some of the reasons she doesn't even bother to ask you about football. So take the opportunity to determine that outcome by setting aside a time to address her questions.

Not every man wants the woman in his relationship to know about football, and that's OK too, but many men find that a woman who not only watches football, but also knows and understands the game, is another reason to find her attractive.

Therefore, if you're a woman, who wants to acquire knowledge, and a man who prefers that the woman in your relationship knows football, this is what needs to happen: your five-step program.

1. For starters, ladies, don't yell out "home run!" when a touchdown is scored (and I don't need to add any explanation for that).

2. If questions arise, wait for the commercials. It's not always the case that he doesn't want to answer you, but unlike golf – which is typically known for its slow play – football has a running on-screen play clock and is played at a very fast pace.

3. When it comes to you asking him questions, it's all about timing. Take notes if necessary, and limit how many questions you ask him at a time. Also understand that the best times to ask questions are when a timeout occurs, during a commercial, when it's halftime, or if there is some other break from the action on the gridiron. You can even ask questions on other days of the week besides

Sundays, when football is on television, and also before or after the season.

4. Don't be intimidated; you may not want to ask what you think is a *dumb question.* Don't let that thought cause a concern. If you want to know something, ask! If you don't feel comfortable asking him, find other ways to get answers.

5. One way is to watch football-related TV programs or websites or hey – you can reach out to me and I'll be delighted to provide some insight – with a woman's touch, of course. I'm available and always willing to help if I can, especially when it comes to football. Of course, I don't know it all, but for the most part, if it's about the rules, the plays/players, or whatever pertains to the games or the sport of football, nothing is off limits. Feel free to contact me via email: ldmiles247@gmail.com with "Football Season" enclosed in the subject line.

If you still prefer to ask him the questions, great! He'll be pleased with the fact that his lady is inquiring about football and he'll be excited about providing you with his insight. He might even react with a silent fist pump or salute you with a kiss, and he might actually exalt with excitement, but don't expect him to blow party horns or throw any confetti about it.

Just keep in mind that he might sound impatient with your questions, but a little bit of that tone is just his shock and happiness. This could also be his first time explaining football to a female, so he could also have some apprehension; remember this is one of the *few* opportunities he gets to be completely right in the relationship. There will still be an air of cockiness during his explanation, but he knows that he definitely can't mess this up, because if he's wrong, his woman will never let him hear the end of it!

Also, keep in mind, that when you prepare to ask him questions, you are dealing with someone who most likely has been involved with the sport of football for the better part of his life. He may have watched football, thrown the football around as a lad or played in little leagues, middle or high school as an adolescent. He might have even coached or played the game in college; and don't let this fool you, he's become a virtual expert through playing those football video games, too.

Depending on the types of questions you ask, he may have to go back to the basics with his answers. That can be a little frustrating for someone who is more advanced on a subject and has to revert to the rudimentary level to explain. But guys, you must be patient and help her. Make sure she isn't intimidated. Break it down to her so that she understands. Put her at ease and don't make her feel dumb ... and don't embarrass her when the two of you are having these conversations.

You can even make it interesting by creating flash cards, testing and challenging each other and playing interactive quiz games. Rather than having an actual coin toss, play a more interesting version of "heads and tails," and make up silly and/or extreme prizes for when she answers correctly.

If you don't have the patience, then I say to you as well: send her to me. I would love to help give her pointers on how to avoid those awkward moments when discussing and watching football. To a certain extent, it can be aggravating for some ladies, knowing that football is televised on other days of the week besides Sundays. Especially when she doesn't understand, or even like the sport, football can become the equivalent of a mistress.

However, football is a multi-billion dollar sport, and it comes with a lot of merchandising, investments, earned capital and media coverage. It captures a great deal of interest from the die-hard fans, both domestic and international. Some of the rules and regulations might change, but with all of the demand and popularity, football isn't going anywhere, anytime soon.

Although much of network TV is dedicated to football and the games around the clock, you can still ensure that the sport does not consume your household. Men, regardless if you are a fan of football, a former player or coach, or you're active, it's important that you don't let football dominate your household during the week. Now if she asks you about football at the dinner table, for example, well, that's different. But still, don't allow it to get out of hand.

Keep the weekday conversations focused on your relationship and your responsibilities within the household. Continue your regular routines, such as checking your kids' homework, going to their games, tournaments and recitals.

You can also discuss other subjects such as your families or work. And guys, definitely don't play video games all week. Granted, video games can help keep you occupied, and yes, we understand that you play against your friends and in online tournaments, but hello ... there's the mortgage to discuss, and you must also keep the spontaneity vibrant in your relationship. Tackle some of those tasks and chores and have them completed before next Sunday's games. You'll be glad you did!

Guys, don't overdo it! Don't take advantage of the fact that football programs and games come on during the week, in addition to Sundays. If you get Sundays to have as your day of relaxation to just watch the games, then don't try to sneak in Mondays and Thursdays or Saturdays too, when college football is also televised.

For those women who already watch the game and have an understanding, that's awesome! You might chime in with your input, but in the midst of making your remarks, just know that one of the worst things you can say during the games is "What happened?"

It's one thing to ask what happened if you turned your head because you sneezed or had to step out the room for a moment. Even when something like that occurs, you can check out the replays, but if you ask what happened during the game, because you don't have a clue, that's a big no-no. Then you've started a war and will definitely get that certain *look* from him. It is imperative to be knowledgeable when discussing football. Knowing what's considered a touchdown is just the beginning. If you're going to give your thoughts, then it's paramount to be aware of what you're talking about.

Being clueless about the difference between the 3-4 base defensive scheme versus the 4-3 structure, or Cover 2, versus Cover 3 is OK. You won't be penalized for not knowing all the proper terminology. That's a little more of the intermediate level of football knowledge, but definitely do learn the difference between when a kicker is setting up to kick a field goal for three points rather than the extra point after a touchdown is scored.

Be on guard; if you see "3rd and 6" in the corner of the television screen, it's great to know that this means the third opportunity for the offense to get a first down and that they need at least 6 more yards toward the goal line to achieve this. If the team on offense obtains the necessary yardage, the set of downs is renewed, beginning with a first down. Do you see how simple that was? Now you're already up one in the plus column.

You might not know that the wide receiver is about to take off from the line of scrimmage to run a skinny post route when the ball is snapped, and that's OK too. But it's a bonus to know that the term "safety" is not only a defensive position in the secondary part of the football field, but it's also a scoring play.

Understand too, that just because the clock indicates 30 seconds remain in the game, you don't actually count down from 30 and think that will end the game. Toward the end of the game, timeouts will be called. There will be additional commercials and strategizing from the coaches and players to extend play as teams within striking distance continue to do whatever it takes to win, until the clock strikes 0:00.

You don't have to know every player's name, what number is on his jersey, what college he attended or his position and duties, but definitely know when to clap and cheer and what teams you are watching. Refrain from saying *the blue team lost today* or *the team with the little birdies on their helmets won.*

Being well informed is the key! It is powerful *and* it is sexy!

This may surprise you men, but some women out there love the sport, just as much as you guys do.

We are also knowledgeable and care about the sport as much as the guys do.

We might even push you to the side during football season!

We are a selected few, but we exist and our population is growing. Get used to it, because we're here, and more of us are coming on board!

06

When Sex & Intimacy
Are Sidelined

When Sex & Intimacy Are Sidelined

In the pre-game portion of this book, I wished the ladies luck in getting the men in their relationships to go out on dates on Sundays during football season. I'm not saying that it's impossible, but it is extremely difficult.

To be completely honest, date nights on Sundays during football season rarely happen! Yes, it sounds obsessive to take football to this extreme. Again, this is not the case for all men and their respective relationships, but typically, they prefer to either go to a game on Sundays or watch the games on television throughout the day.

Nevertheless, there's at least one Sunday during the season when perhaps you will strike oil: the bye week. Ladies, get familiar with his favorite team's schedule, because this will be your "green light" opportunity!

Bye weeks typically begin around the fourth week, in early October, and conclude during week 12 of the regular season, which is toward the end of November.

Most men have a favorite team in the league, and that squad will get a bye and not play a game that particular week. But keep this in mind: men will still want to watch the games because after all, there are other teams to monitor.

Depending on team records and when the bye week occurs, the results of other games could drastically alter what happens to his favorite squad. It may be difficult to pull him away from the TV, but come on guys! You know that *every* game doesn't pique your interest, and if your female counterpart works with you on Sundays during the season, and asks for just that one bye week out of 17, then you can sacrifice.

As with all relationships, guys be ready to make compromises. At least take your team's bye week and dedicate that time to your significant other. Even if it's not the whole day, just make certain that you deliver some romance to her. Plan something while the early games are on TV, during the middle of the day or during the night game. That might make it easier because you have a specified time frame to plan around. If your favorite team played the previous Thursday or doesn't play until Monday night, it's to your advantage to devote time to her on Sunday.

While you're spending that quality time together, it's important to avoid constantly checking your phone or computer for score updates. Fight the urge to keep yourself informed on the latest happenings.

Do not text or resort to social media to find out what's going on with the games either, because you can always get updates later. Regardless, if you go out somewhere or keep the date in a secluded atmosphere at home, make sure the focus is on her.

Even a man's traditional trips to the barbershop on Saturday mornings alter around this time of year. Typically, men prefer to be in and out of the chair. They even go to the extremes of giving the obligatory stand (you know the stand ... they play it off by standing to stretch and/or yawn), but this is an indication to let the other patrons in the barbershop know, that they are next in the chair.

Well, during football season, this still happens; just not all the time.

These changes in the barbershop occur more often when there is a heated debate; for example, who is the greatest running back ever, who were the hardest-hitting defensive players, the banter between divisional foes. As a result, he might sit around the barbershop, just a tad longer than usual, to hear and participate in those *healthy* conversations. This may occur when another patron enters the barbershop with a hat, jacket or even a keychain with a team on it that someone else despises, and that can lead to endless discussions and arguing until your man gets his point across.

Consequently, this elongates the time he spends in there and I would be remiss not to mention that discussions in the barbershop also occur pertaining to the college games slated for that day.

Now to the men, if this occurs, and since your female counterpart has *hopefully* plunged into and embraced her role as your assistant during the season, here is your opportunity to incorporate intimacy, reinstate romance and show her what *else* you're working with.

Perhaps she will be in the salon or spa during your extended visit at the barbershop. Stop by that salon or spa, pay for the services rendered and even bring her some lunch or flowers. This gesture gives her some assurance (and essentially is a nonverbal apology for spending extra time in the barbershop with the guys). It shows that you didn't forget about her; and it puts her on a pedestal in front of other females (and she probably won't admit it, but she'll appreciate that more than you'll ever know). She may even take one or two of those chores from you and handle it herself. Or she may not be as opposed to you watching college football that day, all day, knowing you will be looking at football again the next day, all day. Perhaps, you can help her out at home with some of her chores and additional tasks, since you were in the barbershop longer than usual.

The point is – and as previously discussed – relationships are about balance and compromises, and regardless whether your relationship's status is married, engaged, or just courting, never stop dating your significant other, not even during football season. The dating aspect during this time of year is one thing, but when sexual intimacy is involved, things can get complicated.

Well, actually, sexual intimacy can complicate relationships without football season's involvement, but it's also a little different during this time of year.

OK, so this isn't breaking news, but unless something catastrophic has happened to a man, he will not turn down sex under any circumstances. Well most men, anyway. But when the football games are on, the type of sex that takes place and its frequency can change dramatically. Those days of having sex with ballads playing in the background, candles lit … not while the games are on.

I know, I know!

How in the world can he go from wanting sex so frequently and thinking about it as often as he does during the day – and not always act on it?

Well, watching football can change a man's thought pattern. These are the four different types of sexual activity you can expect during the season: 1. quick and spontaneous with a dash of sidetrack sex; 2. him turning the TV off and actually *participating* during sex; 3. the *calculated* sex; 4. no sex at all.

Here's the breakdown of the "quick and spontaneous with a dash of sidetrack" sex. Keep in mind ladies, the action in football can change in the blink of an eye, and having intercourse while the games are on can be a distraction. His favorite team could be in the red zone, 10 yards away from scoring a touchdown and turn the ball over on the next play.

Now, if he were to miss that play because he was sidetracked and tempted by the sight of your enticing lips, your seductive thighs or any of your other *assets,* he would place blame on you. Of course, he won't tell you that, but it will run across his mind that the turnover happened because he wasn't paying attention to his squad and he let you take his focus instead.

He will most likely communicate that message nonverbally with a certain facial expression of disapproval. Sure, that expression will be because his team turned the ball over, but it's made indirectly toward you.

Therefore, thanks to your body language that aroused him accidentally-on-purpose in the first place, he has intercourse with you in order to keep the peace.

Be careful with your sexual positioning, though. If he faces the TV and your back is toward it, he might be multitasking and watching the game. So if you hear him shout, it might not necessarily be a result of what you're doing to him. I'm not questioning your skills, but you have to take into account that he really wants to watch football, and there may have just been a *score* from the game. I recommend you just wait until all the games are over. But if you don't and you feel a slight disconnection while having intercourse, don't say you weren't forewarned.

Next, for the woman fortunate enough to have her mate participate with her during intercourse …

during the game … and he takes his sweet time … and he actually turns off the television … Congratulations! Your *area* must be dipped in 14-karat gold! You, Ms. Special Lady, might even have the ability to create a secret potion to make Mondays and Tuesdays go by as fast as Saturdays and Sundays.

If he does turn off the TV to have sex with you during the game, then maybe he has a birthday coming up and is working his way up the rankings for a better gift (i.e., some tickets to a football game). Then again, it must be your anniversary, or his team must be getting destroyed or not playing at the time or he might be in the doghouse and this is makeup sex. There must be some agenda!

I'm only kidding! He might be downright horny!

Just make sure your *performance* is worth him missing parts of the game. If not, then he might be even more disappointed in you, than if his team loses that day. You might get a bit of that cold shoulder vibe from him for the rest of the day, so prepare to make up for it. Otherwise, take advantage of his animal instinct and innovate some ways to stimulate his mind while stroking those other areas, as well.

Many women find themselves struggling to get or keep their man's attention because they forget the art of lovemaking. Don't be afraid to speak his language by appearing around the corner dressed in nothing but a towel with his favorite team's logo embossed on it and a stimulating body lotion fragrance. See, now you're massaging his ego as he has the best of both worlds and you're talking under his arena of favorites ... the game to look forward to when he turns the television back on and a sexy woman to match! Football season doesn't have to kill your sex drive. He doesn't have to suffer from withdrawals, and you just might get to unleash the secret freak dwelling within you.

Seriously, enjoy the sex you receive from him while football is on. Of course, football does not (and will not) replace *you,* and while it doesn't make you his side chick, those moments of sacrifice from a man who loves to watch the games deserve some recognition, or even a trophy.

There may also be times when the sex is calculated. It sounds hard to believe that a man would actually schedule sex, right? Nevertheless, during football season, it can and does happen. Besides, don't we always give schedules for him to comply? Exactly! Now it's his turn! It just so happens to occur for him, during the football games.

His appointments to have sex with you will most likely happen during halftime. Intercourse might also take place during pre-game (any time before 1 p.m.), between the first and second session of games (usually at 4:05 p.m.), between the second and third session of games (usually at 7:25 p.m.) and/or during post-game (after the late game around … 11:49 p.m.). Just a reminder, ladies, you will also compete with the highlights throughout the day, from the other teams when they're playing, preliminary reports of games to follow, or the replays of games from the earlier matchups.

Calculated sex, by appointment only, may go longer than a three-minute knockout or unfortunately, it might be a quickie. Remember, he's the one on a schedule and this is not the time to get emotional and demand to have it your way. If it's a quickie, don't act like you've never had one, (or a few, or several) in your lifetime, so don't be alarmed if it happens during football season. Don't suddenly make it a deal breaker for you!

Finally, there is the unbelievable reality that he just might not want sex while the games are on TV. That's not to say that sex will not occur while the games are on, but it's not necessarily his top priority. For the times when you don't fool around while the games are on, do not get discouraged.

Again, it's all about strategy! And you can still have the upper hand. Get your creative juices flowing while he's watching the games, and wait for him to finish. Whip up some chocolate, some strawberries and whipped cream, and save it for later. He might not react right away, but be patient. After he takes a hot shower when the games are over, he's ready for dessert. Surprise him with a hot-oil massage. And never let your feelings ruin an opportunity to release your inner stripper.

Remember this: He's not trying to hurt your feelings; he just wants to watch football without distractions. Put yourself in his shoes ... you love sex and football, but you can only watch the live presentations of football games at specific times. Your lady is sexy, curved in all the right places and naked as a baby's bottom, and you can't have both!

If you play with his senses correctly, he'll also begin looking forward to watching football, just so he can get a taste of you afterwards.

If he does turn you down when you ask him to have sex – or if he doesn't respond when you drop your subtle hints – then it's still OK. Don't get angry, ladies, and definitely don't retaliate. Yes, it can be frustrating, feeling as if you have to compete with some *stupid* football game for his time, attention or sex. And you know how we are as women; we sometimes begin to think, unnecessarily. Men like visual stimulations, and we are the uncontrollable thinkers. We begin to plot and get restless. We think of ways to pull him from that TV, away from watching football, and we get irritated when he doesn't respond.

And you know what's crazy?

Sometimes we may not even necessarily want to have sex with him or seek his attention at that moment. We just don't want to lose to a football game as his source of entertainment, so we start smacking our lips, catching attitudes, crossing our arms, rolling our eyes and using sex as a weapon. Perhaps we do crave his attention and get needy by suddenly playing that damsel-in-distress role. Or, we get more tantalizing and irresistible and give ultimatums. We nag and challenge him, until he succumbs.

Now if you really want the sex, then that's fine.

Otherwise, don't make attempts to lure him from one of his first loves: football. Don't choose to be vindictive just because you don't want him consumed with watching the games. You may inadvertently cause some unnecessary resentment. That's not saying that football is more important than you, but as explained earlier, your objective is to make it through the season emotionally unharmed.

Therefore, if you purposely pull him away from watching football for something that can wait, your intended message may go unheard, and you may end up with your feelings hurt and become offended.

But, what if your strategy works? You get him away from the game. Now what?

Sure, you feel better physically and you're telling yourself, *yeah that's what I thought. He better had stopped watching football. He better had come to me* and you're smirking during the intercourse, just because you *won.* Don't you dare feel boastful or proud, because deep down, you know you're wrong. You've only won the battle, not the war. Ladies, don't do that! Let him have watching his football games, if only for that one day during the week.

There's nothing wrong with being aggressive, and there will be a select number of men who dare you and even prefer that you initiate the move while football is on television, and pull him away from watching the games. But speaking overall, it is highly doubtful. If he's watching football, this is not the time for scheming and manipulation.

I reiterate: it's only football, and he just really wants to watch the games. He doesn't find you any less attractive or less desirable, it's just that he has that unique and unbreakable bond with the sport, and his attention is focused on what's happening on the field.

Watching football does not warrant sentencing him to sleeping on the couch. Don't fret; it's not another woman. The only mistress in this case is a football game.

The results of the games can also dictate what type of sex will or won't happen during football season. Expect him to have some sexual frustration if his favorite team loses. And if his team wins, he might go on a spending spree. What may also determine his reactions is what took place in his fantasy football league(s). How he responds to you when his favorite team wins could be identical to when his team loses. Or, his reactions could be at separate ends of the spectrum.

However, the more common response if his favorite squad is victorious is that he will want extra-special attention. That may include and is not limited to an extra round of sexual activity. See, he didn't forget about you, all he wanted was to watch the games, and now you can top off his day with some victory sex. Now it's time to work it, main-chick-style, and let him know you're running the show. With the games over, transform that living room or man cave into your own little halftime entertainment stage. Try getting into some new and different positions and let him tackle you. Let your man play the role of the game-winning quarterback and you're at the press conference waiting to present him with a signing bonus and an MVP award. Or, set up the bathroom and create a faux-pas scene, act out the plot as if you're worried about getting caught having sex in the locker room to add some adventure.

Definitely don't dress in a pair of "stay away from me" pajamas and destroy the mood. Continue to sport your lace, your teddies and your heels too, but change it up sometimes and throw on a cheerleading uniform. Remember that earlier in this book, I informed you about the incredible women's attire embossed with team logos. Therefore, wear something with his favorite team's logo on it. In fact, dress up in his favorite team's jersey … but just the jersey and heels, with no undergarments.

This next example to spice up the mood: Combine some lacy lingerie (designed in his favorite team's colors), with a teddy or even some boy shorts, heels and a hat with his favorite team's logo embossed on it (Now I don't know about a helmet with his favorite team's logo on it, but hey

… to each its own). He'll probably be watching the highlights in another room, especially if his team won, so seeing the replays of how the victory was achieved never gets old to him. Light some chamomile candles in the bedroom and turn on some ballads or even some music that represents the sound of victory.

Hold the hat on the sides of the brim and pull it down over your eyes for a mysterious look. Slink into the room where he's watching TV, dressed in your heels and skimpy attire. Do a little sexy routine to the rhythm of the music by gyrating, swaying your hips, biting your bottom lip, etc. Pull on the brim of the hat, and then throw up a little point to the team logo on it. You don't even have to say his team won, but that sexy, subtle point to the logo on the hat lets him know that you know. Line up in victory formation and well, you can use your imagination to know what happens next!

For the most part, men are easy to please, and this gesture is a simple way of showing that you paid attention. Again, men like visuals, while we women are the thinkers. Paint a picture for him! It shows him that you were focused and thinking.

All of these examples are tips, key components in your relationship of keeping his interest, keeping him excited, and staying on your duties as his main chick, particularly during football season. Don't ask him if you can do this, and don't even wait for him to ask you. Just go ahead and do it!

Typically, guys make the first move, but it is definitely OK to take the initiative sometimes and this is a perfect illustration of when to do so. It's an incredible feeling to finish your entire day victoriously, so why not top off this triumphant occasion for him?

On the flipside, when his favorite team loses (this is especially the case with the championship game), he may still want intercourse, but it'll be nothing special. You really don't have to do too much, other than show up and participate. At this moment, he may be upset and just wanting to relieve some frustration. Having intercourse with him may even clear his head, so please, try not to refuse.

Some do's and don'ts apply to this special situation. Definitely don't wear anything with his favorite team's logo on it. Any reminders of the loss are unnecessary. In fact, don't even talk about the loss for the rest of the week.

In case he doesn't want to have sex, just try to make things as smooth and soothing around the house as possible (i.e. preparing some comfort food). You want to see a man's emotional side? His favorite team losing will bring it out of him. Ladies, he has his personal reactions and own version of PMS, realizing his favorite team *Probably Might Suck!*

He may be distant, distracted and unresponsive, but it will pass. Don't take it personal if he acts a little more reserved around the house. He probably won't answer his phone or respond to text messages, not necessarily because it's from another woman he's avoiding while you're around, but because it's some of his buddies on the other end.

Of course, they want to remind him of the loss and they want to talk about those bets they made and ask him for their money. Those types of calls will be sent straight to voicemail, ignored, or he'll just hang up on them. He might answer their calls, and it'll be surprising if he takes the defeat and lets them torment him about his favorite team's loss. He's prone to raise his voice at these moments, and there'll be some banter – and he'll probably use some profanity – as he exclaims his frustration to the other end of the phone. He might discuss what went wrong in the game or what could've been done differently. Now these conversations will most likely occur with a buddy who roots for the same team as he does.

See ladies, another part of the reason why he will become so distant is because he has to prepare for work in the morning and face his coworker(s). For starters, it's about to be a Monday morning. Secondly, I can almost guarantee they were talking smack to each other on Friday and over the weekend, placing bets, saying this or that will happen in the game, and so forth.

In addition, the water cooler talk on a Monday morning can be brutal if your favorite team loses, especially if your coworker(s) cheer for a team that just defeated your squad, the day before. Also because of Monday night football games, water cooler talk can be even worse on Tuesday mornings, especially if you lost in fantasy football to someone that you work with and have to face them.

Somebody might just get fired, and you definitely don't want it to be your man!

So, there you have it ... some assurance for the women, with a feminine touch, some explanation on the men's behalf and some understanding for both genders. The scales are balanced, and after this recap, you should be good to go, ready and set, to watch and enjoy some football!

POST-GAME COVERAGE

Post-Game Coverage

Relationships are hard work. If they were easy, then everyone would have them. For many women, going through football season with a man who loves the sport and dedicates so much time to watching the games can be a very challenging aspect to sustaining a relationship. Believe me, I've heard your stories and I get it!

I hope both parties can get something from this literary work and know what to expect when this time of year comes around. The main thing is, don't panic! You will get through this tough time together and possibly grow stronger because of going through it together. The content in this book isn't life-saving, but it is designed to help you smooth over the rough spots and save your relationship. That's no guarantee that you will be together forever though. Other issues aside from him watching football will arise and challenge your foundation, but it's my hope that this book can assist by creating a balanced and happy medium during the season.

If you do have debates and arguments, you can definitely use this book as a tool to make your point on how relationships can survive the annual onslaught of football season.

I've given you some tips, some backup assistance in trying to be constructive within your relationship. Let this book be a resource to restore teamwork, and start a dialogue about football season. Now, let's recap and make sure we're all on the same page.

Sports are typically a major part in a man's life, especially football. Many have played the game, coached the game, or had another type of participation in some shape, form or fashion in the sport, so please forgive these men for their fascination and passion for football.

In addition, men have a huge admiration and the utmost respect and appreciation for the game, as well as its players and coaches. Yes, that infatuation can be an issue, and it's highly doubtful that it will break your own relationship, but it's something that needs more discussion. Use the content in this book as a guide when you find yourself stuck during football season.

What is his silence saying? How do you gain or secure your rightful place as his main chick?

I'm trying to open the lines of communication on this subject because women are looking for ways to be more relatable to the men in their relationships. Dialogue is one way to achieve your goal.

To the ladies, your man loves you dearly, but he also loves football. The types of love are different, but he is not choosing football over you. In fact, there is no choice for him to make. He just wants to escape for a little while and watch the games on Sundays.

The word of the day is *sanctuary*. That's what football is for him. You don't have to become defensive or dislike football season because he's devoting more time to what's going on within the sport. Football is not your enemy and you're not being replaced. After all, football season won't wash his clothes or prepare him any dinner. Football season won't even tie his necktie or satisfy any of his other needs, so he still needs you to be his sexy queen! He just also needs his *sanctuary*.

With every relationship come some sacrifices and football season can truly test those boundaries.

Because watching football is important to him (and so are you), becoming his ally and joining forces with the season can be rewarding. It can strengthen you individually, along with your collective bond within your relationship. Being his ally can eliminate some unnecessary tension and keep some peace in your household during the season. Perhaps it will even create a better dialogue in your relationship throughout the year.

Ladies, if you follow the tips mentioned in this book, it does not make you weak, submissive or too accommodating. From checking the television service and remotes, to shopping for merchandise with team logos on it for him, to understanding and accepting that he will play fantasy football, to allowing him to watch the larger, flat-screen TV while the games are on. Don't nag him while the games are on. You will lower your own blood pressure by simply leaving him alone. Understand that the time he spends in the barber shop might be extended and acknowledge the difference in his behavioral patterns when it comes to communicating and having sex, and intensifying your sexual prowess and creativity for him during the season. All these acts of compassion (or you might call it catering to him!) actually make you more compatible.

Now men, it's also up to you to create a balance between your two loves to help take some of the edge off, especially if and when your female counterpart feels estranged. It is still your duty to be the provider and the comforter amongst other duties as the man in your relationship. Continue to go to the gym, work and/or go to school, take care of your lady, your children, your family and the household inside and out.

Make time for her, help her out more often around the house, and show your gratitude for her sexuality and her efforts to please you. Never stop dating the woman in your relationship, and appreciate the fact that she is trying to adapt to your culture of watching football. Try to communicate with her more often, handle your financial obligations, and continue to participate in your religious activities. Don't use football season as an excuse to avoid your obligations at home. If you do, then don't watch next Sunday's games, plain and simple. Address your other priorities first!

Although results from some of the football games may cause you to shut down, you are not entitled to shut her out. Do not make her feel alienated just because she isn't into the sport as much as you are. Just because football is *your thing,* she knows she can compromise, but you are not to be put on a pedestal. And if she wants to learn about football, then you teach her patiently and in a manner that doesn't make her feel inferior to your expertise. No snickering allowed!

Ladies, you will be just fine, because you're not the side chick, *football season* is.

The season is just some convenient, temporary enjoyment for him, only allowed to come around once a year for about 22 weeks, and it's gone within approximately 150 days. It's a short-term affair, lasting less than six months, and maybe – just maybe – his favorite team will capitalize on its nominal 3.125 percent chance of winning the game of the season on football's biggest stage and earn a ring. Now that will give him something to brag about.

During this time of year, there's no doubt that your man is preoccupied with watching the games, but ladies, I assure you, football season zooms by faster than summertime, and before you know it, *she* will be gone! Football season is followed by the spring and summer portions of the offseason, and then the attention is completely back where we want it ... all on us!

Thanks to our bathing suits, sundresses, shorts, skirts and dresses that allow us to show off our legs, and our pedicures. As for our shoes ... well, it'll be time for open-toe season! We get to pull from the stash in our secret shoe closets, and you know we'll have him help us again; to haul in those delivered boxes from our online shopping sprees or extra bags from the department stores when we go shopping for more footwear.

The regular season for football is just four months, and five months tops, when you factor in the playoffs. The championship game is on the first

Sunday in February and that concludes the season. Get ready to get sexy!

Hang in there ladies! With this perfect timing, once the championship game is over, it's all worth it in the end. Your man will still have 7 to 13 days to go out and shop … for your Valentine's Day gifts!

AUTHOR'S CORNER

Author's Corner

Listening to the way LaTasha D. Miles talks about sports, you would think she doesn't leave home without her football. Her love for the game is evident in her background, expressions, and personality.

Born and raised in ACC country, the bubbly dose of brown sugar never had the goal to fit in, but to stand out, growing up surrounded by male cousins and uncles in Burlington, N.C. and developing into a tomboy. Outnumbered by the males, LaTasha had no choice but to join them as they gathered around that one television at "grandma's house" after church for Sunday dinner and football.

At first, LaTasha disliked the sport, but she found herself eager to learn more about the game, and did just that by pestering others to explain the rules and regulations. She began researching, learning formations, coaching trees, schemes and all things related to the sport. The more she watched football, the more her love for the sport increased.

Football had found a new fan in LaTasha D. Miles.

Her quest for knowledge about the sport afforded her opportunities to write, edit, co-host, host, produce, broadcast as a radio personality and as a sideline reporter. As a sports journalist, LaTasha has landed several front-page articles with interviews from Hall of Fame members including Bobby Bowden, Terry Bradshaw and Dick

MacPherson. In addition to interviews with defensive end William Hayes of the Miami Dolphins, ESPN's own Stephen A. Smith, the only living Negro League Baseball umpire, author Robert "Bob" Motley and BMX phenomenon Brett "Mad Dog" Banasiewicz, she graduated Magna Cum Laude from Winston-Salem State University in Winston-Salem, N.C. LaTasha earned a Bachelor of Arts degree in mass communications, with a concentration in sports journalism.

A standout in sports writing and sports editing, she earned accolades in both lines of work and covered baseball, basketball, golf, soccer, tennis, and of course, football, in Indiana, North Carolina, Tennessee and Washington D.C. Now having emerged as the self-proclaimed *dainty tomboy* – and with her heart of gold and big smile in tow – LaTasha is ready to hit the mainstream level in the sports reporting and broadcasting realms.

Featured in magazines and on local and national television stations more than 35 times, the author has also moved into positions of branding that are more creative. Affectionately known as "Joan Madden, The Gridiron Goddess", LaTasha also created *SheSPN The Network* and *WTF Too: Women Talk Football Too,* which both display a broader range of her passion, knowledge, personality and charisma while discussing football and other sports and returning to her sports writing roots.

Who knew that a little girl without any interest in football would become one of its biggest fans, so full of vigor and always prepared for a challenge?

In addition to football, LaTasha is an enthusiast for fashion, interior decorating, traveling, volunteering and is a fanatic of choreography and listening to music, especially Beyoncé.

LaTasha enjoys bowling and swimming, and absolutely adores full-blooded Boxers and children. Her love for God, family and friends, and helping others are at the center of what keeps her grounded.

www.ingramcontent.com/pod-product-compliance
Lightning Source LLC
Chambersburg PA
CBHW030013110426
42741CB00032B/483